CW01508690

DESH EXPRESS LTD

Stranger Things
The Novelization of Season Two

Copyright © 2025 by Desh Express LTD

All rights reserved. No part of this publication may be reproduced, stored or transmitted in any form or by any means, electronic, mechanical, photocopying, recording, scanning, or otherwise without written permission from the publisher. It is illegal to copy this book, post it to a website, or distribute it by any other means without permission.

First edition

*This book was professionally typeset on Reedsy.
Find out more at reedsy.com*

To the dreamers who find courage in the unknown,
and to every reader who believes that stories have the power
to connect us across worlds both real and imagined.

"Sometimes the strangest places lead us to the truest parts of ourselves."

Contents

Foreword

This book is a work of passion born from admiration for stories that blur the line between the ordinary and the extraordinary. While inspired by the themes of courage, friendship, and resilience found in beloved shows and novels, this is an independent reimagining - a fan inspired retelling crafted for readers who enjoy exploring familiar worlds through fresh perspectives.

It is important to note that this work is not affiliated with, endorsed by, or connected to Netflix, the Duffer Brothers, or any official Stranger Things property. Instead, it is a transformative homage created to celebrate the enduring spirit of storytelling.

Preface

Stories have always been a way for us to face the shadows and step into the light. When I began this project, I wanted to capture the feeling of suspense, wonder, and discovery that comes from stepping into a world where ordinary people confront extraordinary challenges.

This book is not meant to replace or replicate any official material. Instead, it offers a new voice, shaped by imagination, admiration, and the shared joy of storytelling. My hope is that readers find within these pages echoes of what they love, while also encountering something original and unexpected.

Thank you for joining me on this journey. May it spark your own adventures into the strange and the unknown.

Acknowledgments

No story exists in isolation. I would like to thank:

- The readers who open their hearts to new interpretations and fan-inspired storytelling.
- The creative works that first lit the spark of imagination and showed us the beauty of friendship, courage, and resilience.
- Friends and family who encouraged me to keep writing when the road felt uncertain.
- And most importantly, you the reader. Without your curiosity and support, these words would remain silent on the page.

One

The Aftermath

Fall had settled over Hawkins, Indiana, painting the town in a palette of deep oranges, golds, and browns. Leaves crunched beneath the feet of children who frolicked on their way to school, the crisp air imbued with the promise of Halloween. But for Will Byers, the world outside felt muted, as if he were trapped in a sepia-toned photograph. The vibrant colors of autumn faded into the background, overshadowed by the darkness that haunted him.

Will had been home for a few months now, but the trauma of his experiences in the Upside Down clung to him like a heavy fog. At night, the shadows in his room morphed into grotesque shapes, and he found himself waking in cold sweats, heart racing, the remnants of nightmares still clinging to him. He would see it the shadowy figure looming over him, its presence suffocating. It was the Mind Flayer, a creature born of nightmares, and it had etched itself into his mind.

"Will, sweetheart, it's time to get ready for school!" Joyce called from the kitchen, her voice laced with concern. She had tried everything to help her son heal, from late-night talks to warm cups of cocoa, but nothing seemed to alleviate the weight he carried. She was fiercely protective, a lioness guarding her cub, but the limitations of her understanding left her feeling helpless.

"Okay, Mom," Will replied, forcing a smile that didn't quite reach his eyes. He pushed the covers off and sat up, glancing around his room, the walls adorned with posters of heroes and fantastical worlds, yet feeling more like a cage than a sanctuary.

As he dressed, his mind drifted to the therapy sessions Joyce had insisted upon. He had sat across from a woman Dr. Owens who had asked him endless questions about his feelings, his nightmares, and his time in the Upside Down. He wanted to tell her everything, to articulate the terror that clawed at him from the inside, but the words always faltered at the edge of his tongue. How could he explain the visions? The way the Mind Flayer seemed to seep into his thoughts, whispering dark promises of control and despair?

"Will!" Joyce's voice broke through his reverie, and he hurriedly finished getting ready.

At breakfast, the tension was palpable. Joyce tried to engage him in small talk, but Will offered only half-hearted responses, his mind elsewhere. "You should talk to your friends today," she suggested, trying to bridge the gap between them. "Maybe Mike can help you feel better."

"Yeah, maybe," he mumbled, pushing his cereal around the bowl. The thought of facing Mike, Dustin, and Lucas felt heavy. They had shared so much, but how could he explain that he felt like he was still trapped in the Upside Down, even when the physical danger had passed?

As the school bus pulled up, Will took a deep breath and stepped outside. The chill in the air felt sharper today, and he wrapped his arms around himself as he boarded the bus. His friends were already seated, animatedly discussing the latest episode of their favorite sci-fi show, Star Wars. Their laughter felt distant as he took a seat beside Mike, who looked up with a smile that quickly faded into concern.

"Hey, Will," Mike said softly, his eyes searching Will's face for signs of the friend he once knew. "How are you doing?"

"Fine," Will lied, forcing a smile. He could see the worry etched into Mike's brow, the way Dustin and Lucas exchanged glances, clearly unsure of how to help. The truth was that he wasn't fine not at all.

As the bus rattled down the familiar streets of Hawkins, Will felt the weight of his anxiety pressing down on him. He watched the trees blur by, their branches reaching out like skeletal fingers. The school loomed ahead, a place of refuge and pain, filled with memories of friends and laughter that felt tainted by the darkness of his past.

Inside the school, the hallways buzzed with the chatter of students, but Will felt detached from it all. He walked with Mike, Dustin, and Lucas, who were animatedly discussing their Dungeons & Dragons campaign. It was comforting, a reminder of happier times, but as they reached their lockers, the familiar faces of their classmates and the laughter that echoed around them only served to amplify Will's isolation.

"Hey, do you want to play D&D later?" Lucas asked, trying to draw Will into their camaraderie. "We can go to the Byers' and set up the game. It'll be fun!"

"Yeah, I'll think about it," Will replied, forcing the words out. The thought of diving into their fantasy world offered a flicker of hope, a distraction from the shadows creeping into his mind. But the reality of his visions loomed like a storm cloud overhead.

As the school day dragged on, Will found himself lost in thought, his mind drifting to the dark figure that haunted him. In class, he doodled in his notebook, sketching the silhouette of the Mind Flayer, its massive, spider-like form looming over him, its eyes filled with malice. He wanted to scream, to tell someone, but the fear of what he might unleash kept him silent.

Finally, the school day came to an end, and he gathered with Mike, Dustin, and Lucas at the bus stop. "You coming over?" Dustin asked, his usual enthusiasm shining through. "You've gotta see the new monster I created for D&D!"

Will hesitated, glancing back at the school, its walls feeling like a prison. "Yeah, I'll come," he said finally, the desire for normalcy outweighing his fears.

As they walked to the Byers' house, laughter and chatter filled the air, but Will felt the weight of an unseen burden, the dark whispering of the Mind Flayer echoing in his mind. He pulled his jacket tighter around himself, steeling himself for the battle ahead both with his friends and within himself.

When they arrived at the Byers' house, Joyce greeted them with a warm smile but quickly sensed the tension in Will's demeanor. "Hey, guys! Want some snacks?" she called as they entered, trying to lighten the mood.

"Sure!" Dustin replied, already rummaging through the kitchen. As the boys settled down with snacks and their D&D setup, Will tried to immerse himself in the game, but the shadows lurking in his mind refused to be ignored.

As the game progressed, however, he felt the familiar thrill of adventure return. They crafted their characters, strategized their moves, and for a moment, Will felt like a kid again a kid who had not just survived the Upside Down but had friends to share the experience with. But as the game grew more intense, Will's vision blurred, and he was suddenly pulled back into the darkness.

The Mind Flayer's voice echoed in his mind, a sinister whisper that sent shivers down his spine. "You cannot escape. I am coming for you."

"Will?" Mike's voice broke through his trance, concern etched on his face. "Are you okay?"

"I... I'm fine," Will stammered, but the certainty in his voice faltered. He looked around at his friends, their faces a mixture of worry and determination. They were his lifeline, and he knew he had to fight for them.

"Let's keep playing," he said, forcing a smile as he grasped the dice in his hand. But deep down, he knew that the true battle was just beginning.

Two

New Friendships

In the weeks following Will's return to school, the air in Hawkins grew colder, signaling the approach of winter. The trees stood bare, their branches skeletal against the gray sky, and the townsfolk prepared for the holiday season, but the children of Hawkins were still grappling with the shadows of the past.

Mike, Dustin, and Lucas had grown closer as a group, their bond forged in the fires of previous adventures, but a new presence had entered their lives Max Mayfield. The new girl was a whirlwind of energy, her skateboard tucked under her arm and a confident smile on her face. She had quickly become a part of their group, but her arrival also marked the beginning of new dynamics among them.

"Come on, Max, roll the dice!" Dustin shouted, his usual enthusiasm infectious as they gathered in the Wheeler basement for another Dungeons & Dragons session. The atmosphere was electric, filled with laughter and friendly banter, but Mike felt a nagging sense of unease. He couldn't shake the feeling that they were still on the cusp of something dark.

"I'm not just going to roll it," Max replied, her fiery spirit shining through as she shot Dustin a playful glare. "I need to know the consequences first! What happens if I roll a one?"

"Then you'll fall off your skateboard and land in a pile of Demogorgon guts!" Lucas chimed in, earning a laugh from the group.

"Gross!" Max exclaimed, her laugh ringing out like music. Despite her initial reservations about fitting in, she quickly proved her intelligence and bravery, impressing the boys with her strategic thinking and bold moves in the game. It wasn't long before Lucas developed a crush on her, a fact that did not go unnoticed by Mike and Dustin.

As the game progressed, Mike found himself glancing at Max more frequently, captivated by her confidence and quick wit. It was strange, watching Lucas flirt with her, a mix of admiration and jealousy bubbling beneath the surface. He knew he shouldn't feel this way after all, he was still holding out hope for Eleven but the reality of her absence weighed heavily on him.

"Hey, Mike, you still there?" Dustin nudged him, breaking him from his thoughts. "You're going to have to help me defeat this monster. You're the Dungeon Master!"

"Right, yeah... sorry," Mike replied, shaking his head and trying to focus. He glanced down at his notes, but his thoughts drifted back to Eleven. He wondered what she was doing, whether she was safe, and if she was thinking of him too.

As the game continued, Max's laughter filled the room, her energy infectious. "Okay, I'm ready! What's my next move?" she asked, her eyes sparkling with excitement.

"You see the Demogorgon ahead," Mike explained, slipping into his role with enthusiasm. "It's blocking the path to the treasure. What do you do?"

"I charge at it!" Max declared, her confidence shining through. "I'm not afraid of some overgrown lizard!"

"Alright, roll for initiative!" Mike grinned, impressed by her bravery. He watched as Max rolled the dice, and the room erupted in cheers as she succeeded in her attack.

But just as the game reached a thrilling climax, Will's expression shifted, the laughter fading as he felt the familiar weight of dread settle in. The whispers began again, growing louder in his mind. "Will…" the voice echoed, dark and menacing. "You cannot escape."

"Will?" Mike's voice broke through the fog, concern etched across his face. "Are you okay?"

"I… I'm fine," Will replied, forcing a smile, but the unease lingered. He could feel the connection to the Mind Flayer tightening, a vice grip on his thoughts. He couldn't let it show; not now, not in front of his friends.

"Hey, let's take a break," Lucas suggested, sensing the tension. "How about some snacks?"

"Good idea!" Dustin exclaimed, jumping up to grab the chips. The group made their way to the kitchen, the echo of laughter returning as they filled their plates.

As they settled back around the table, Max leaned closer to Will, her curiosity shining through. "What do you think about our campaign so far?" she asked, her voice warm and inviting. "You've been really quiet."

"Yeah, it's cool," Will replied, forcing a smile. "I like how you're not afraid to take risks."

Max grinned, her confidence infectious. "Thanks! I think it's important to be bold. Life's too short, right?"

"Right," Will echoed, the warmth of her presence pushing back against the darkness that threatened to consume him.

As the night wore on, Will felt a flicker of hope. Perhaps, in this group, he could find a way to confront the shadows lurking in his mind. Perhaps he could allow himself to connect with his friends again.

But as the laughter filled the room, a chill ran down Will's spine. He could feel the Mind Flayer's influence lurking just below the surface, waiting for the right moment to strike. He knew he had to stay vigilant, for the battle was far from over, and the darkness was always watching.

Three

The Return of Eleven

The world outside felt colder as winter approached, the first snowflakes dusting the ground and transforming Hawkins into a winter wonderland. But for Eleven El it was a stark reminder of the isolation she felt while hiding away with Jim Hopper. The warmth of the fireplace in their shared cabin could not thaw the coldness of her separation from Mike and the rest of her friends.

Hopper had tried his best to create a semblance of normalcy for El. He taught her how to cook, helped her navigate the world outside, and even introduced her to the simple joys of playing board games. But despite his efforts, El felt the pull of her past the memories of Hawkins, of her friends, of the life she had once known. She missed the laughter, the adventures, and especially Mike, whose absence weighed heavily on her heart.

"Eleven," Hopper called from the kitchen, breaking her out of her thoughts. "Want to help me make dinner?"

El forced a smile and nodded, wanting to please him. As she joined him in the kitchen, she noticed how different everything felt how normal it was. But the normalcy felt foreign to her, an uncomfortable reminder of what she had lost.

"Can you pass me the salt?" Hopper asked, focused on the stove.

El reached for the salt shaker, her fingers brushing against it, and in that moment, a flash of memory surged through her mind Mike's face, bright with laughter, the warmth of their friendship wrapping around her like a comforting blanket. She missed him fiercely.

"Hey, are you okay?" Hopper asked, noticing her faraway gaze. "You seem a bit distracted."

"Just thinking," El replied softly, her voice barely above a whisper. "About my friends."

Hopper turned to her, concern etched across his face. "I know it's hard. But you need to stay safe. The lab is still looking for you, and I can't let them find you again."

"I can't hide forever," El said, her voice trembling with emotion. "I need to see them. I need to know they're okay."

Hopper sighed, rubbing the back of his neck. He understood the longing in her heart, the desire to reconnect with the people who had accepted her for who she was. "I get it, El. But right now, it's not safe. We need to wait until I'm sure it's clear."

Frustration boiled inside her. She wanted to scream, to break free from the confines of her life in hiding. But she couldn't. She was trapped, and the walls felt like they were closing in.

Later that night, as Hopper watched TV in the living room, El retreated to her room. She lay in bed, staring at the ceiling, her thoughts swirling with memories of her friends. The laughter, the adventures, the shared battles against the darkness it all felt like a dream.

As she closed her eyes, the memories began to flicker before her, and she felt a deep yearning. Suddenly, she had a vision a brief glimpse of Mike, Dustin, Lucas, and Will gathered around the table, their faces etched with worry. The familiar warmth of friendship washed over her, pulling her closer to the surface of her emotions.

Then, she saw a shadow lurking in the background, a dark figure that sent chills down her spine. It was the Mind Flayer, and it was watching Will. Panic surged through her as she opened her eyes, her heart racing. She couldn't ignore the connection any longer.

"I have to go back," she whispered to herself, determination igniting within her. She needed to return to Hawkins, to protect her friends from whatever darkness awaited them.

The next morning, El made her decision. She began gathering supplies clothes, food, and anything she could use to make the journey back into Hawkins. She knew she had to be quick; Hopper would never agree to her leaving, but she couldn't let that stop her.

As she prepared to leave, she felt a mix of fear and excitement. The world outside was vast, filled with unknown dangers, but she was ready to face them. She had survived the horrors of the Upside Down; she could survive this.

When Hopper left for work, El took her chance. She slipped out of the cabin and into the woods, her heart pounding with every step. The cold air bit at her skin, but she pushed forward, fueled by the hope of reuniting with her friends.

The journey back to Hawkins felt endless, but as she approached the familiar town, memories flooded back the laughter, the warmth, the camaraderie. She could almost hear Mike's voice calling her name.

Once she reached the outskirts of town, she paused, feeling a mix of trepidation and excitement. The streets of Hawkins were quiet, but she could sense the tension in the air. Something was off.

El made her way toward the Wheeler house, her heart racing. She needed to see Mike, to let him know she was back. But as she approached, she felt a dark presence lurking in the shadows, the cold grip of fear tightening around her heart.

Will's face flashed in her mind, the way he had looked during their last encounter haunted and terrified. She had to protect him, to help him fight the darkness that threatened to consume him.

With newfound determination, El stepped onto the porch of the Wheeler house and knocked on the door, her heart pounding in her chest. She had returned, but she was not just the girl they had known before. She was stronger, wiser, and ready to face whatever awaited her.

As the door creaked open, she was met with the familiar face of Mike Wheeler, his eyes widening in disbelief. "El?" he whispered, his voice barely audible, as if he feared she would disappear again.

"Mike," she breathed, and in that moment, all the fears and uncertainties melted away. She was home.

Four

The Mind Flayer's Influence

The early signs of winter descended upon Hawkins, wrapping the town in a blanket of frost. The festive decorations adorned the streets, but beneath the surface, an unsettling tension lingered. Will's nightmares had intensified, and the whispers had grown louder, intertwining with his waking thoughts like tendrils of darkness.

"What do you mean you're seeing things?" Joyce asked, her voice trembling with concern as they sat in their living room, the glow of the lamp casting shadows across the walls. Will fidgeted with his hands, the anxiety palpable in the air.

"I don't know, Mom. It's just… there's this shadow," he replied hesitantly, searching for the right words. "It's always watching me. I keep seeing it, and it feels like it's inside my head."

"Is it the same shadow you saw before?" Joyce pressed, her heart racing. "The one from the Upside Down?"

Will nodded, his gaze dropping to the floor. "It feels different this time. It feels... more powerful."

Joyce felt a wave of dread wash over her, but she fought to remain calm for Will's sake. "We need to talk to Hopper about this," she said, determination lacing her tone. "He'll know what to do."

Just as Joyce was about to reach for the phone, the front door swung open, and Mike, Dustin, Lucas, and Max burst into the house, their laughter filling the air.

"Hey, Will! We're going to have a D&D marathon!" Dustin exclaimed, his energy infectious. "We need you to help us defeat the Mind Flayer!"

"Yeah, we've got some new ideas for our campaign!" Lucas added, grinning widely.

Will's heart sank as he glanced at his friends. He wanted to join them, to escape the weight of his fears, but the shadow loomed larger in his mind. "I... I can't," he said quietly. "Not today."

The joy on his friends' faces faltered, replaced by concern. "Will, what's wrong?" Max asked, her voice gentle. "You can't keep shutting us out."

"I'm just tired," Will replied, forcing a smile that didn't quite reach his eyes. "It's been a long week."

"Come on, we'll make it fun!" Dustin insisted, his optimism unwavering. "Besides, we can't let the Mind Flayer win, right?"

Will looked at his friends, their faces filled with encouragement. He wanted to believe that they could conquer anything, even the darkness that threatened to engulf him. "Okay, I'll try," he said, finally relenting.

As they gathered around the table, the familiar setup of game pieces and character sheets brought a sense of comfort. Mike took on the role of Dungeon Master, his enthusiasm palpable as he guided them through their adventure. But even as the game unfolded, Will found it hard to focus. The shadow in his mind grew stronger, whispering insidious thoughts that clawed at his resolve.

"Will, roll for initiative!" Mike called, breaking through Will's haze. He glanced at the dice in front of him, but all he could see was the darkness creeping into the edges of his vision.

"I… I don't think I can," he admitted, his voice shaking. "I keep seeing it."

"Seeing what?" Lucas asked, concern etched on his face. "Will, you need to tell us. We're here for you."

"The Mind Flayer," Will admitted, his voice barely above a whisper. "It's watching me. It wants something."

The room fell silent, the weight of his words sinking in. Dustin shifted uncomfortably, glancing at Mike, who looked equally concerned. "Will, we beat the Mind Flayer before. We can do it again," Mike said, trying to sound reassuring.

"But what if it's different this time?" Will replied, his heart racing. "What if it's stronger?"

"Then we'll be stronger too," Max said firmly, her voice full of conviction. "We faced down the Demogorgon together; we can face this too."

Will met her gaze, searching for the strength he desperately needed. He wanted to believe her, to feel the camaraderie that had once felt so solid. But the shadow in his mind continued to gnaw at him, an insidious presence that refused to be ignored.

As the game continued, Will felt himself slipping further away from reality. The lines between the game and the shadows began to blur, and he could feel the Mind Flayer's influence creeping into his thoughts. It wanted him to succumb, to give in to despair.

Suddenly, the lights flickered, and the air grew heavy. Will looked around, panic rising in his chest. "Guys, something is wrong," he said, his voice trembling.

Before anyone could respond, a chilling breeze swept through the room, extinguishing the candles and plunging them into darkness. Will felt the rush of fear, the shadows closing in around him. "It's coming!" he shouted, his heart racing.

"Will, focus!" Mike urged, trying to keep his friend grounded. "We're here with you. Remember our plan!"

"Will, you're the strongest of us all!" Lucas added, his voice firm. "You can fight it!"

As the shadows twisted and writhed, Will felt the grip of the Mind Flayer tighten around his heart. He could almost hear its voice, dark and menacing. "You are mine, Will. You cannot escape."

"No!" Will shouted, shaking his head fiercely. "I won't let you take me!"

In that moment of defiance, a flicker of light pierced through the darkness a memory of El, of her unwavering strength, surged to the forefront of his mind. He thought of their friendship, of the battles they had fought together, and he summoned all his courage.

"I am not alone!" Will cried, and as he did, he felt a surge of energy course through him. In a whirlwind of determination, he grasped the tabletop, grounding himself in reality.

The lights flickered back on, and the shadows receded, leaving behind the familiar warmth of the room. Will looked around at his friends, who stared at him with wide eyes, their expressions a mix of awe and concern.

"Will, are you okay?" Max asked, her voice trembling.

"I'm… I'm okay," he replied, though the weight of the Mind Flayer's influence still lingered in the corners of his mind. "But it's not over. It's still out there."

The group exchanged worried glances, the reality of their situation settling heavily upon them. They knew they had to confront this darkness, but they also understood that it would take more than just bravery; it would take unity, trust, and the strength of their friendship.

As they resumed their game, a newfound determination filled the air. They would face the Mind Flayer together, and no darkness would tear them apart. The battle had only just begun, and Will was ready to fight for himself, for his friends, and for the light that still flickered in the shadows.

Five

Dart and Discovery

The first snow had fallen in Hawkins, transforming the town into a winter wonderland. Children bundled in coats and scarves rushed outside to build snowmen and engage in snowball fights, their laughter ringing through the crisp air. But inside the Henderson household, Dustin Henderson was preoccupied with something much more peculiar than snow.

"C'mon, Dart, don't be shy!" he called, crouching down to coax the small creature out from behind the couch. Dart, his newfound pet, was a strange little critter resembling a baby Demogorgon though Dustin was convinced he was just an adorable anomaly.

But Dart was more than just a pet; he was a mystery that Dustin was eager to unravel. "You've got to eat something, buddy!" he insisted, holding out a piece of leftover pizza. Dart peered out, his big eyes glistening with curiosity, and finally scuttled forward, sniffing at the food.

Dustin's heart swelled with pride. "That's it! You're going to be the coolest pet ever!"

Just then, the door swung open, and Lucas and Max entered, shaking off snow from their clothes. "Hey, Dustin! You ready for our D&D session?" Lucas called out, but as he caught sight of Dart, his expression turned to concern. "What is that?"

"It's my new pet!" Dustin exclaimed, puffing out his chest. "His name is Dart, and I think he's going to be the best monster in our campaign!"

"Dart? Like the game?" Max asked, raising an eyebrow, but curiosity sparkled in her eyes.

"Yeah, but it's short for 'Demogorgon,'" Dustin explained, his enthusiasm unwavering. "He's not just any creature; he's special!"

As Dustin continued to ramble about Dart's potential, Lucas exchanged a worried glance with Max. "Are you sure it's safe to keep him? I mean, remember how things went with the last Demogorgon?"

"Come on, guys! He's just a baby!" Dustin protested, bending down to scratch Dart's head. The creature let out a soft chirp, and Dustin grinned. "See? He's harmless!"

But as the trio settled down to play D&D, Dart remained a source of distraction. The game unfolded, and the atmosphere was lively, filled with laughter and banter, but Dustin couldn't shake the feeling that something was off. Dart's behavior had become increasingly erratic, and he often seemed to stare off into the distance, as if sensing something beyond the walls of the house.

"Alright, guys, I'm the Dungeon Master this time!" Max declared, her excitement palpable. "We're going to face the Mind Flayer!"

As the game progressed, Dustin struggled to focus, darting glances at Dart, who was now nibbling on a piece of pizza. "Hey, you alright, buddy?" Dustin asked, noticing the creature's strange behavior. Dart's eyes glinted with a curious light, and he let out a sound that resembled a whimper.

"Dustin, focus!" Lucas urged, trying to keep the game moving. "We can't let the Mind Flayer win!"

"Right, right!" Dustin replied, shaking his head. He tried to immerse himself in the game, but Dart's odd behavior kept pulling at the edges of his concentration.

After the game, the trio settled into the living room to eat snacks and chat. "You think Dart is okay?" Dustin asked, glancing down at the creature.

Lucas shrugged, a hint of concern still lingering. "I don't know, man. He seems kinda... weird."

"Maybe he's just hungry?" Max suggested, her brow furrowed as she watched Dart curiously.

Dustin sighed, feeling a mix of protectiveness and worry. "I'll take care of him. I just need to keep an eye on him."

As they continued to talk, Dart suddenly bolted, darting out of the room and into the hallway. "Dart! Come back!" Dustin shouted, scrambling to follow.

"Where is he going?" Lucas asked, concern growing as they ran after him.

They found Dart in the kitchen, pawing at the door that led to the basement. Dustin's heart raced; he had never taken Dart down there, fearing what might happen if he did. "What are you doing?" Dustin asked, kneeling beside the creature.

But Dart seemed insistent, scratching at the door with an urgency that sent chills down Dustin's spine. "Fine, let's see what you want," he muttered, opening the door and leading the way downstairs.

The basement was dimly lit, filled with the remnants of family memories and dust-covered boxes. Dart scurried ahead, his movements quick and erratic, sniffing the air as he went. "Dart, wait up!" Dustin called, following closely behind.

As Dart reached the far corner of the basement, he paused, staring intently at the wall. "What are you looking at?" Dustin asked, his voice quivering slightly.

Then, without warning, Dart let out a high-pitched chirp and began scratching at the wall, as if trying to dig through. "Dart, stop!" Dustin shouted, panic rising within him. "What are you doing?"

"Dustin, maybe we should get out of here," Lucas said, his voice tense. "I don't like this."

"No, wait! He's trying to tell us something!" Dustin insisted, kneeling beside Dart. "There's something here! We have to find out what it is!"

With renewed determination, Dustin began to search the area, feeling the wall for hidden panels or loose bricks. Just as he was about to give up, he noticed a small crack near the baseboard. "Guys, come help me!" he called, excitement filling his voice.

With Lucas and Max's help, they pried at the crack, and to their astonishment, a section of the wall shifted. A hidden compartment opened, revealing a small cache of items strange vials, broken equipment, and a faded photograph of a group of scientists gathered around a table.

"What the…?" Lucas breathed, his eyes wide. "What is all this?"

Dustin picked up the photograph, examining it closely. "This looks like it was taken at Hawkins Lab," he said, his heart racing. "Maybe it's connected to everything that happened last year."

Max peered over his shoulder, reading the faded name on the back of the photo. "It says Dr. Brenner. He's the one who experimented on El, right?"

"Yeah, and he's the reason we had to fight the Demogorgon," Dustin replied, a sense of unease settling over him. "What if there's still stuff down here from the lab? What if they're still doing experiments?"

Suddenly, Dart let out a low growl, the hairs on the back of his neck standing on end. The trio exchanged worried glances, realizing they were not alone.

"Guys…" Lucas whispered, his voice trembling. "I think we need to get out of here."

But before they could react, a chill swept through the basement, the temperature dropping suddenly. The shadows seemed to swirl around them, creeping closer, and the air grew thick with an unsettling energy.

Dart's eyes widened, and he let out a frantic chirp as he darted back toward the stairs. "Wait, Dart!" Dustin shouted, but the creature was already gone, racing up the steps.

"Let's go!" Max urged, her voice urgent. They scrambled to follow Dart, but as they reached the top of the stairs, the door slammed shut behind them, trapping them in darkness.

"Dustin!" Lucas shouted, panic rising in his voice. "What's happening?"

23

"I don't know!" Dustin replied, trying to push against the door, but it wouldn't budge. "We have to find another way out!"

The shadows began to close in around them, the air thickening with an ominous presence. The whispers of the Mind Flayer echoed in Dustin's mind, a chilling reminder that the darkness was still out there, lurking, waiting for the right moment to strike.

As the group huddled together, fear coursing through their veins, they realized that the battle against the Mind Flayer had only just begun, and the shadows of the past were once again threatening to consume them. With Dart's connection to the Upside Down growing stronger, they had to act quickly before it was too late.

Six

Uncovering the Truth

The following days in Hawkins were filled with a sense of foreboding. The first real snow had fallen, blanketing the town in white while the darkness seemed to seep into the very fabric of their lives. Will's visions intensified, and Dustin's discovery of Dart had left the group with more questions than answers.

Joyce and Hopper were drawn together by their determination to protect their children, but the shadows of the past continued to loom large. They met in Joyce's living room, poring over the scattered notes and drawings Will had made, trying to piece together the puzzle of the Mind Flayer.

"Joyce, we need to consider the possibility that the Mind Flayer is coming back for Will," Hopper said, his brow furrowed with concern. "We've seen the connection before, and it feels like it's getting stronger."

"I know," Joyce replied, her voice trembling as she glanced at Will, who sat quietly in the corner, his eyes distant. "But how do we stop it? What if it's not just targeting him this time?"

Hopper leaned back in the chair, running a hand through his hair. "We have to find out what's happening at the lab. There must be something they left behind, something that can give us a clue about the Mind Flayer's intentions."

Just then, the door swung open, and Dustin, Lucas, Max, and Mike entered, their expressions a mixture of excitement and fear. "You won't believe what we found!" Dustin exclaimed, practically bouncing on his feet.

"What is it?" Joyce asked, her heart racing.

"We found some stuff in Dustin's basement that might be linked to Hawkins Lab," Lucas said, urgency in his voice. "But we think Dart might be connected to whatever is going on."

"Dart?" Hopper echoed, raising an eyebrow. "What do you mean?"

Dustin pulled out the photograph they had discovered, holding it up for everyone to see. "Look at this! It's a picture of Dr. Brenner and some scientists. We think they were working on something related to the Mind Flayer!"

Hopper leaned forward, studying the photograph closely. "If they were experimenting with the Upside Down, it could explain how the Mind Flayer is gaining power again. We need to get this to the authorities."

"No!" Will suddenly said, his voice sharp. "If we tell them, they might just try to shut everything down. We need to handle this ourselves."

Joyce's heart sank at the determination in Will's eyes. She could see the shadows of fear that clung to him, but she also felt the strength of his resolve. "Will, we need to keep you safe, but we can't fight this alone."

"We can do it together," Mike said, stepping forward. "We know how to face these things. We've done it before."

As the discussion continued, Will's mind raced with visions of the Mind Flayer, the shadows looming larger and larger. He could feel the entity's influence creeping closer, like a fog that threatened to engulf him. "We need to go to the lab," he said suddenly, his voice steady. "If there's a way to stop it, we have to confront it head-on."

The group exchanged glances, uncertainty flickering in their eyes. "It's dangerous," Max cautioned. "What if we're walking into a trap?"

"But what if we don't do anything and it gets worse?" Dustin argued. "We have to take the risk if we want to protect our town."

Hopper sighed, weighing the options. "If we're going to do this, we need a plan. We can't just walk in without knowing what we're up against."

That night, they gathered in the Wheeler basement, armed with flashlights and determination. They spread out maps of Hawkins Lab, drawn from memory and past experiences, and began to strategize.

"Okay, we'll split into two teams," Hopper suggested. "One group will distract any guards outside while the other sneaks in to gather information. We'll meet back at the Byers' house afterward."

As they finalized their plans, Will's heart raced. The connection to the Mind Flayer felt stronger than ever, a dark presence whispering in his mind. He needed to confront it not just for himself, but for his friends.

The next day, as the group prepared to head to the lab, Will felt a mix of anxiety and determination. They arrived at the outskirts of Hawkins Lab, the imposing building standing like a sentinel against the gray sky. Its walls bore the scars of time, but the air was thick with tension, and Will could feel the shadows closing in.

"Are you ready?" Mike asked, his expression serious as he met Will's gaze.

"Yeah," Will replied, steeling himself. "We have to do this."

They split into their two teams, with Hopper, Joyce, and the kids moving cautiously toward the entrance. The atmosphere was charged, and the whispers in Will's mind grew louder as they approached.

As they neared the entrance, they spotted movement inside the familiar figures of scientists bustling about, unaware of the impending confrontation. Will's heart raced as he felt the Mind Flayer's presence lurking in the shadows, watching.

"Remember the plan," Hopper whispered, his voice steady. "Stay alert."

The group moved with stealth, slipping inside the building. The stark lights illuminated the sterile hallways, casting eerie shadows. Will felt the weight of the darkness pressing down on him, a reminder that they were stepping into the heart of the beast.

"Over here!" Lucas called, pointing to a door marked "Research." They approached cautiously, Will's heart pounding as they prepared to push the door open.

As they entered, a chill ran through the air. The room was filled with monitors and equipment, the remnants of experiments long forgotten. Will's breath caught in his throat as he scanned the room, the memories flooding back the pain, the fear, the darkness that had once consumed him.

"Look at this!" Dustin exclaimed, pointing to a series of files stacked on a desk. "These are research notes about the Upside Down!"

"Grab them!" Hopper urged, his eyes scanning the room for any signs of danger.

But just as Dustin reached for the files, the lights flickered and dimmed, plunging them into darkness. The air grew cold, and Will felt the presence of the Mind Flayer surge, wrapping around him like a vice.

"Will!" Mike shouted, grabbing his arm. "Stay with us!"

The whispers grew louder, filling Will's mind with chaos. "You are mine," the Mind Flayer hissed, its voice dark and seductive. "You cannot escape."

"No!" Will shouted, shaking his head as he fought against the grip of the entity. "I'm not yours!"

Suddenly, the lights flickered back on, and the group stood frozen as a shadowy figure began to materialize in the center of the room. It was the Mind Flayer, its massive form looming over them, a dark embodiment of all their fears.

"Will, you have brought them to me," it hissed, its voice echoing through the chamber. "You cannot protect them from the inevitable."

"Get back!" Hopper shouted, stepping forward protectively. "We won't let you take him!"

As the Mind Flayer's tendrils reached out, Will felt a surge of strength rise within him. He looked at his friends Mike, Dustin, Lucas, Max and knew they had to fight together. "We can do this!" he shouted, determination blazing in his eyes. "Together!"

With that, the group rallied around Will, their friendship forming a shield against the darkness. They fought back against the Mind Flayer, using the strength of their bond to push back against the shadows threatening to consume them.

As the battle raged on, Will felt the connection to the Mind Flayer weaken, the shadows receding as their combined light shone brighter. They were not just friends; they were warriors, standing united against the darkness.

With one final surge of energy, they cast the Mind Flayer back into the shadows, the darkness dissipating like smoke. The room fell silent, the air heavy with the remnants of their battle.

As they stood together, panting and shaken, Will felt a sense of relief wash over him. They had faced the darkness and emerged victorious at least for now.

But deep down, he knew the battle was far from over. The Mind Flayer would return, and they would have to be ready. Together, they would confront whatever came next, for their friendship was the light that would guide them through the darkest of times.

Seven

The Showdown

As Halloween approached, Hawkins was a town caught in the grip of festivity and fear. The streets were adorned with pumpkins and cobwebs, children dressed as ghosts and goblins filled the sidewalks, and the air buzzed with excitement. But beneath the surface, an unease lingered, a reminder of the darkness that had threatened to consume them.

Will's visions had become more intense, each night bringing a clearer image of the Mind Flayer a towering, spider-like creature that loomed over Hawkins, its shadow stretching across the town. His friends tried to reassure him, but the connection felt stronger than ever, and he knew they were running out of time.

"We need to make a plan," Mike said, gathering the group in the Wheeler basement. "The Mind Flayer is coming for us, and we have to be ready."

"I think we should use the D&D campaign to strategize," Dustin suggested, his enthusiasm shining through. "We can pretend the Mind Flayer is a boss monster and figure out how to defeat it!"

"That's a great idea!" Max chimed in, her eyes lighting up. "We can develop a strategy based on our characters' strengths."

As they set up for the game, Will felt a mix of excitement and dread. They had faced challenges before, but this felt different. The stakes were higher, and the darkness was closer than ever.

As the game began, Mike took on the role of the Dungeon Master, guiding them through their adventure. "You find yourselves in a dark forest, the air thick with tension. The Mind Flayer lurks in the shadows, watching your every move."

As the players rolled their dice and crafted their strategies, Will felt the weight of his fears pressing down on him. The Mind Flayer was not just a monster in their game; it was a powerful entity that threatened to take over their lives.

"Will, what do you want to do?" Mike asked, drawing Will back into the game.

"I want to scout ahead," Will said, his voice steady. "I want to see what we're up against."

As Will's character moved forward, he felt a surge of energy. He was no longer just a pawn in the game; he was a part of the story, fighting against the darkness. The familiar camaraderie of his friends surrounded him, and he felt the warmth of their support.

But as the game progressed, the atmosphere grew tense. The shadows in the room seemed to shift, and the whispers began again, echoing in Will's mind. "You cannot escape, Will," the Mind Flayer hissed. "You are mine."

"No!" Will shouted, shaking his head as he fought against the darkness. "I won't let you take me!"

His friends exchanged worried glances, and Mike stepped forward, determination in his eyes. "Will, you're not alone. We're here with you."

With each declaration of support, Will felt the grip of the Mind Flayer weaken, the shadows receding as their friendship formed a protective barrier. They were stronger together, and they would face this darkness head-on.

As they continued their game, the tension in the air began to lift. They strategized, planned their moves, and fought back against the Mind Flayer with the strength of their bond. It was a battle of wits and courage, and they were determined to emerge victorious.

But just as they reached a critical point in the game, the lights flickered, and the room grew cold. Will's heart raced as the familiar presence of the Mind Flayer surged back, creeping into his thoughts. "You cannot win," it hissed, its voice echoing in his mind.

"Will, focus!" Mike urged, his voice steady. "We can do this together!"
    With a surge of determination, Will closed his eyes, visualizing the strength of his friends surrounding him. "I am not alone!" he shouted, and as he did, the darkness began to recede, the light of their friendship pushing back against the shadows.

With one final push, they unleashed their combined strength, casting the Mind Flayer back into the darkness. The air grew warm again, and the whispers faded, leaving behind a sense of peace.

As the game ended, the group sat in silence, the weight of their battle settling upon them. They had faced the Mind Flayer and emerged victorious but they knew the darkness was not gone forever.

"Will, are you okay?" Max asked, concern etched on her face.

"I'm okay," Will replied, though he could feel the lingering shadows in his mind. "But we have to stay vigilant. It's not over yet."

The group nodded, understanding the urgency of their situation. They had faced darkness before, but they would continue to stand together, united against whatever challenges lay ahead.

As Halloween night approached, the excitement in Hawkins grew, but for Will and his friends, a sense of foreboding lingered. The Mind Flayer was still out there, watching, waiting for the right moment to strike. They had fought bravely, but the true battle was yet to come, and they would need to rely on each other to face the darkness that threatened to consume them all.

Eight

The Battle for Will

Halloween arrived in Hawkins with a crisp bite in the air and the excitement of the season buzzing through the streets. Children dressed as ghosts, witches, and superheroes filled the sidewalks, their laughter mingling with the rustling of leaves. But for Will, the festive atmosphere felt like a façade, a thin veil over the darkness that was creeping closer.

As night fell, the group gathered at the Byers' house, the familiar warmth of friendship surrounding them. The air was thick with tension as they prepared for the ultimate confrontation with the Mind Flayer. Will's visions had intensified, the entity's presence looming larger than ever, and they knew they had to act fast.

"Okay, guys, this is it," Mike said, his voice steady as he addressed the group. "Tonight, we're going into the Upside Down to confront the Mind Flayer. We have to save Will before it's too late."

Will's heart raced at the thought of facing the creature that haunted his dreams. "What if it's too powerful? What if it takes me again?" he asked, fear creeping into his voice.

"You're not alone, Will," Lucas reassured him, placing a firm hand on his shoulder. "We're all in this together. We've faced down monsters before, and we can do it again."

Dustin nodded, his usual bravado shining through. "Yeah! We've got our D&D strategy, and we know how to fight. Plus, we have Dart on our side!"

"Dart?" Will echoed, glancing at Dustin. "What does he have to do with this?"

Dustin smirked, a glint of mischief in his eyes. "Trust me. If Dart can sense the Mind Flayer, we'll know when it's close."

With their plan set and their resolve strengthened, the group gathered their supplies flashlights, walkie-talkies, and whatever weapons they could find in the Byers' basement. Will felt a surge of determination as he looked at his friends, knowing they would face this darkness together.

As they made their way to the woods, the atmosphere grew heavy with anticipation. The trees loomed around them, their branches clawing at the sky like skeletal fingers. The shadows felt alive, whispering secrets that sent shivers down Will's spine.

"Stay close," Hopper instructed, his voice low and authoritative as he led the way. "We don't know what we're up against."

The group moved cautiously, the sounds of the night punctuated by the crunch of leaves beneath their feet. Will could feel the connection to the Mind Flayer growing stronger, a dark presence that seemed to be watching them from the shadows.

As they reached the clearing where the portal to the Upside Down had once been, Will felt a surge of fear. "It's here," he whispered, glancing at his friends. "I can feel it."

"Get ready," Mike said, his voice steady as he raised his flashlight. "We need to be prepared for anything."

With that, they stepped into the darkness, the world around them shifting as they crossed into the Upside Down. The familiar landscape morphed into a twisted reflection of Hawkins, shadows swirling around them like a dark cloud.

"Is everyone okay?" Max asked, her voice trembling slightly as she looked around at the distorted world.

Will nodded, though his heart raced. The air felt thick with tension, and he could sense the Mind Flayer's presence lurking just beyond their sight. "We have to stick together," he urged, feeling the weight of the darkness pressing down on him.

As they navigated through the Upside Down, the whispers grew louder, echoing in Will's mind. "You cannot escape," the Mind Flayer hissed, its voice a chilling reminder of the battle ahead. "You will be mine."

"No!" Will shouted, shaking his head fiercely. "I won't let you take me!"

As they moved deeper into the shadows, the group began to split up, each person scouting for signs of the Mind Flayer's presence. Will felt a growing unease, an instinctive awareness that something was about to happen.

Suddenly, Dart appeared, darting through the shadows and making his way toward Will. "Dart!" Dustin called, his voice filled with excitement. "What is it, buddy?"

But Dart stopped suddenly, his body tense as he sniffed the air. A low growl rumbled in his throat, and Will felt the hair on the back of his neck stand on end. "Dart senses something," he said, his heart racing.

Before they could react, the shadows coalesced into a massive form the Mind Flayer materialized before them, towering and menacing, its eyes glowing with dark intent. "You have come to me," it hissed, its voice echoing through the Upside Down. "You cannot resist."

"Will!" Mike shouted, stepping forward protectively. "Stay back!"

But the Mind Flayer turned its gaze toward Will, a malevolent grin spreading across its face. "You are weak, Will. You belong to me!"

"No!" Will shouted, fighting against the darkness that threatened to consume him. He could feel the grip of the Mind Flayer tightening around his mind, the whispers growing louder, but he refused to succumb. "I am not yours!"

With a surge of determination, Will focused on his friends, their presence grounding him in the chaos. "I'm not alone!" he shouted, and as he did, he felt a wave of energy radiate from their bond, pushing back against the darkness.

The Mind Flayer recoiled, the shadows swirling around it like a storm as it fought to maintain its hold. "You think you can resist me?" it hissed, anger seeping into its voice. "You will suffer!"

"Not if we can help it!" Lucas shouted, brandishing a makeshift weapon he had fashioned from a broken branch. "We're not afraid of you!"

As the group rallied together, the power of their friendship surged, forming a shield against the darkness. Will felt the connection to his friends strengthen, their collective determination pushing back against the Mind Flayer's influence.

"Together!" Mike urged, his voice steady. "We can do this!"

With that, they charged forward, their hearts united in the face of the darkness.

Will felt the light of their friendship shining brightly, illuminating the shadows that threatened to engulf them.

As they confronted the Mind Flayer, the battle raged on, a clash of light and darkness echoing through the Upside Down. The power of their bond surged, pushing back against the entity that sought to control them, fighting against the darkness that had threatened to consume them all.

With one final push, they unleashed their collective strength, driving the Mind Flayer back into the shadows. The darkness began to recede, the whispers fading into silence as they emerged victorious at least for now.

As the dust settled, Will felt a wave of relief wash over him. They had faced their fears and emerged stronger, but he knew that the battle was far from over. The Mind Flayer would return, and they would have to be ready.

As they stood together in the Upside Down, Will felt the warmth of their friendship surrounding him, a reminder that no darkness could extinguish the light they shared. They would continue to fight, united against whatever challenges lay ahead, for their bond was unbreakable, and together, they would face the darkness that threatened their town.

Nine

Sacrifices and Revelations

The aftermath of the battle against the Mind Flayer resonated through the air, leaving a heavy silence in its wake. The group stood in the Upside Down, their hearts racing as they processed the intensity of what they had just faced. Will could still feel the lingering presence of the Mind Flayer, but the darkness had retreated for now.

"Is everyone okay?" Max asked, her voice trembling as she glanced around at her friends.

"I think so," Lucas replied, his face pale but determined. "But we need to get out of here before it comes back."

Dart scuttled over to Dustin, nuzzling against his leg as if sensing the tension. "Good boy, Dart," Dustin said, bending down to pet him. "You helped us fight back."

As they prepared to leave the Upside Down, Will felt a surge of emotion. He was grateful for his friends, for their bravery and support, but he also felt the weight of the darkness that lingered. He knew the Mind Flayer wouldn't stay gone for long it wanted him, and it wouldn't stop until it had him.

"Will?" Mike said, noticing the distant look in his friend's eyes. "Are you alright?"

"I don't know," Will admitted, fear creeping into his voice. "I can still feel it, you know? The Mind Flayer's presence is still there, even if it's not here right now."

"We need to figure out what it wants," Hopper said, his voice steady. "If it's targeting you, we have to understand why."

As they stepped back into Hawkins, the familiar sights of the town felt both comforting and unsettling. The shadows of the Upside Down lingered, a reminder of the darkness that had threatened to consume them.

"Let's regroup at the Byers' house," Joyce suggested, her voice firm. "We need to come up with a plan."

Once they arrived back at the Byers' house, the atmosphere was tense with anticipation. They gathered around the table, a mix of snacks and uneaten Halloween candy strewn about, remnants of the festivities that felt so distant now.

"Okay, let's go over what we know," Joyce said, her tone serious. "The Mind Flayer is still out there, and it has a connection to Will. We need to figure out how to sever that connection."

"I think it's using Will as a way to control us," Dustin said, glancing at Will. "It wants to manipulate him, to make him its vessel."

Will nodded, feeling the weight of their words. "I can feel it trying to pull me in, to make me its puppet. It's like it knows my thoughts, my fears."

Max leaned forward, her brow furrowed in concentration. "What if we could use that connection against it? If we know what it wants, we can find a way to fight back."

"Right, but how do we do that?" Lucas asked, concern etched on his face. "We've never faced anything like this before."

"There's something we haven't tried yet," Mike said suddenly, his eyes lighting up. "What if we could communicate with the Mind Flayer? If we can get it to reveal its intentions, maybe we can find a way to weaken its hold on Will."

The room fell silent as they considered the idea. Will felt a mix of fear and determination. "But what if it tries to take me again? What if I can't fight it?"

"We'll be with you," Dustin assured him, his voice steady. "No matter what happens, we'll face it together."

As the group strategized, Will felt a surge of hope. They were united, ready to confront the Mind Flayer head-on. But deep down, he knew that the battle would require sacrifices, and he wasn't sure if he was prepared for what lay ahead.

As the night wore on, Will found himself lost in thought. The darkness still lingered in his mind, and he could feel the Mind Flayer's influence trying to claw its way back in. He needed to stay strong, to fight back against the shadows that threatened to consume him.

The next day, they began their preparations, gathering supplies and creating a plan to confront the Mind Flayer. Will felt the weight of their mission bearing down on him, but he was determined to protect his friends no matter the cost.

As they set out to face the Mind Flayer once again, Will could feel the shadows closing in. The whispers grew louder, echoing in his mind. "You will be mine," the Mind Flayer hissed, its voice a chilling reminder of the darkness that awaited them.

But Will refused to give in. He would fight back, drawing strength from his friends and the bond they shared. Together, they would confront the Mind Flayer and uncover the truth behind its sinister intentions.

As they approached the site of the battle, Will took a deep breath, steeling himself for what lay ahead. The shadows loomed around them, but he could feel the warmth of his friends beside him, a beacon of light in the darkness.

"Let's do this," he said, determination shining in his eyes. "Together."

Ten

A New Beginning

The aftermath of the climactic battle against the Mind Flayer left Hawkins in a state of cautious optimism. The snow-covered streets were adorned with holiday decorations, and the air buzzed with excitement as families prepared for the upcoming festivities. But for Will and his friends, the memories of their fight lingered, a reminder of the darkness they had faced and the bonds they had forged.

The group gathered at the Byers' house, a sense of relief washing over them as they reflected on their victory. They had confronted the Mind Flayer and emerged stronger, but the scars of their experience remained.

"Can you believe we did it?" Dustin exclaimed, a wide grin on his face. "We actually fought the Mind Flayer and won!"

"I'm just glad we're all okay," Max said, her eyes shining with relief. "I was really worried there for a while."

Will sat quietly, absorbing the warmth of their camaraderie. He felt a mix of gratitude and uncertainty. Although they had defeated the Mind Flayer, he could still feel its lingering presence in the back of his mind—a dark shadow that refused to fade away completely.

"Will, you okay?" Mike asked, noticing Will's contemplative expression.

"Yeah, I'm fine," Will replied, forcing a smile. "I'm just...thinking."

"About the Mind Flayer?" Lucas asked, concern etched on his face.

"Kind of," Will admitted, his heart heavy. "I just... I don't want to go back to that darkness. I don't want it to find me again."

Joyce entered the room, sensing the tension. "Is everything alright?" she asked, her maternal instincts kicking in.

"We were just talking about the Mind Flayer," Mike explained. "Will's worried it might come back."

Joyce knelt beside Will, her expression softening. "You don't have to be afraid, sweetheart. We're here for you, and we'll always protect you. You're not alone."

Will nodded, appreciating his mother's reassurance. But deep down, he knew that the battle against the darkness was not just external; it was internal as well. He had to confront his fears head-on.

"Maybe we can do something to honor our victory," Max suggested, breaking the somber mood. "What if we have a celebration? We can invite everyone from school, and make it a Halloween to remember!"

"Yeah!" Dustin exclaimed, his face lighting up. "A party! We can show everyone that Hawkins is still standing strong!"

The idea sparked excitement in the group, and as they began to plan the celebration, Will felt a sense of hope blossom within him. Perhaps this was the fresh start they needed a chance to celebrate their friendship and the strength they had found in each other.

As preparations for the party moved forward, the group rallied together to decorate the Byers' house. They hung strings of lights, arranged pumpkins, and set up games, each task reinforcing their bond as friends. Laughter filled the air, and for the first time in a long while, Will felt a sense of normalcy wash over him.

The night of the party arrived, and the house was transformed into a festive wonderland. The scent of popcorn and candy filled the air, and the sounds of laughter echoed through the halls as their classmates arrived, eager to join in the celebration.

Will stood by the door, greeting guests and feeling a wave of gratitude wash over him. He watched as his friends mingled, their smiles brightening the room. Mike and Max played a game of charades, while Dustin and Lucas set up a make-your-own candy station.

As the night wore on, Will felt lighter, the shadows receding as laughter and joy filled the air. He knew that the darkness would always be a part of him, but in this moment, he felt a renewed sense of hope. They had faced the Mind Flayer together, and they had emerged victorious.

As the clock struck midnight, the group gathered for a toast. Hopper raised his glass, his eyes shining with pride. "To friendship, courage, and the strength of our community. We've faced darkness before, but together, we can overcome anything."

The room erupted in cheers, and Will felt a surge of warmth. They were united, ready to face whatever challenges lay ahead. As he raised his glass, he looked around at his friends Mike, Dustin, Lucas, Max, and Joyce and felt a sense of belonging wash over him.

In that moment, he realized that the battle against darkness would continue, but as long as they stood together, they would always find a way to fight back.

As the celebration continued, the laughter echoed through the Byers' house, a testament to their resilience and strength. They had faced the darkness, and though it would always linger, they were ready to embrace the light together.

Epilogue

The Impending Darkness

As winter settled over Hawkins, the town transformed into a picturesque landscape of snow-covered rooftops and twinkling lights. The holiday spirit was alive, but beneath the surface, an unsettling feeling lingered. The Mind Flayer may have been temporarily vanquished, but its shadow still loomed over the town.

Will stood at the window of the Byers' house, watching as snowflakes danced through the air. He felt a sense of peace after the party, but the whispers in his mind had not disappeared completely. The connection to the Mind Flayer still pulsed within him, a dark reminder of the battles they had fought.

"Will, come look at this!" Dustin called from the living room, breaking Will from his thoughts. He turned to see his friends gathered around the television, their faces lit with excitement.

"What is it?" Will asked, moving closer to see the screen.

"It's a news report about Hawkins!" Lucas exclaimed, pointing to the television. "They're talking about the strange occurrences happening in the area."

As the news anchor spoke about unexplained phenomena and bizarre sightings, Will felt a chill run down his spine. The Mind Flayer's influence was still present, lurking just beneath the surface. He exchanged worried glances with his friends, knowing that the battle was far from over.

"Do you think it's a sign?" Max asked, her voice filled with concern.

Will nodded, his heart heavy. "I think it means we have to stay vigilant. The Mind Flayer might return, and we need to be ready."

As the news report continued, the camera panned to the woods surrounding Hawkins, the shadows stretching ominously across the landscape. Will could feel the darkness calling to him, a reminder that the battle against the unknown was far from finished.

"Together, we can face it," Mike said, his voice steady. "We've done it before, and we can do it again."

Will turned to his friends, determination igniting within him. "Yeah, together," he affirmed. "No matter what happens, we'll always have each other."

As they stood together, united in their resolve, the whispering shadows continued to swirl around them, a reminder of the darkness that threatened their town. But with their friendship as their guiding light, they were ready to face whatever challenges lay ahead.

The battle against the Mind Flayer was just the beginning, and they would stand together, prepared to confront the impending darkness. Together, they would fight, for Hawkins, for their friends, and for the light that would guide them through the shadows.

As the snow continued to fall outside, the warmth of friendship enveloped them, a beacon of hope in a world filled with uncertainty. They would face whatever came next, united in their strength and unwavering in their determination. The fight was far from over, but they were ready for the challenge.

Printed in Dunstable, United Kingdom

70730783R00037